IMPLEMENTATION OF DISCLOSURE IN FEDERAL DISTRICT COURTS, WITH SPECIFIC ATTENTION TO COURTS' RESPONSES TO SELECTED AMENDMENTS TO FEDERAL RULE OF CIVIL PROCEDURE 26

DONNA STIENSTRA
RESEARCH DIVISION
FEDERAL JUDICIAL CENTER

MARCH 1, 1994

On December 1, 1993, amendments to the Federal Rules of Civil Procedure went into effect. Among these, amendments to Rule 26 provide for three types of self-executing disclosure: initial disclosure; expert disclosure; and pretrial disclosure. The amended rule also provides for deferral of formal discovery until parties have met to discuss and plan discovery and to make or arrange for the exchange of disclosures.

The proposed amendments to Rule 26 generated substantial controversy and an effort, ultimately unsuccessful, to persuade Congress to remove the proposed changes from the rule. The rule itself permits each court by local rule or order to exempt all cases or categories of cases from some of the rule's requirements and also permits parties to stipulate out of some of the requirements.

Since the effective date of the amendments, interest has been high in the courts' responses to amended Rule 26. How many have "opted out" of the rule's requirements, as the practice has come to be known? The attached tables summarize the courts' responses to selected parts of the amended rule by showing which subdivisions of the rule are in effect in each district and which are not.[1] The tables also show whether districts in which the federal rule is not in effect require disclosure through local rules or the Civil Justice Reform Act plan.[2] As we will see, without this information a simple count of courts opting out of the Rule 26 amendments would understate the adoption of disclosure in the federal courts.

To aid the user of these tables, in the sections below we briefly describe the rule amendments addressed by the tables, then note how the tables may be read, and finally identify some of the patterns in the courts' responses to Rule 26(a).

Description of Selected Amendments to Federal Rule of Civil Procedure 26

Rule 26(a)(1), Initial Disclosure. Except as otherwise stipulated or as directed by order or local rule, a party must provide, without awaiting a discovery request, the following information at or within ten days of the meeting of counsel required by Rule 26(f):

---

[1] The information is current as of February 23, 1994 and will be updated at an appropriate point.
[2] The Civil Justice Reform Act of 1990 (28 U.S.C. §§ 471-482) requires each federal district court to adopt a cost and delay reduction plan by December 1, 1993. All courts have adopted a CJRA plan.

- name, address, and telephone number of all persons likely to have discoverable information relevant to disputed facts alleged with particularity in the pleadings, with identification of the subjects of the information;
- a copy or description by category and location of all documents, data compilations, and tangible things in the party's possession, custody, or control that are relevant to disputed facts alleged with particularity in the pleadings;
- computation of damages claimed, with supporting documentation to be available for copying or inspection; and
- insurance policies that may satisfy the judgment, to be available for inspection or copying.

Rule 26(a)(2), Expert Disclosure. Parties must disclose the identity of persons who may testify as experts at trial **[(a)(2)(A)]** and, except as otherwise stipulated or as directed by the court, must provide a written report prepared and signed by the expert **[(a)(2)(B)]** containing:

- a complete statement of all opinions to be expressed by the expert and the basis for them;
- the data or other information considered by the expert in forming the opinions;
- exhibits to be used to summarize or support the opinions;
- qualifications of the expert;
- compensation to be paid the expert; and
- a list of cases in which the expert has testified at trial or by deposition in the last four years.

In the absence of other directions by the court, disclosure of experts must be made at least 90 days before the case is to be ready for trial or within 30 days of another party's disclosure when intended only to contradict or rebut that disclosure.

Rule 26(a)(3), Pretrial Disclosure. A party must provide the following information about the evidence it may present at trial other than solely for impeachment purposes:

- name, address, and telephone number of each witness, separately identifying those the party expects to call and those it may call if necessary;
- list of witnesses whose testimony is expected to be presented by deposition and, if the deposition was not taken stenographically, a transcript of the pertinent portions; and
- a list or categorization of documents or other exhibits, including summaries of evidence, separately identifying those the party expects to offer and those it may offer if necessary.

Unless otherwise directed by the court, these disclosures must be made at least 30 days before trial. Within fourteen days of this disclosure, certain objections [specified in the rule] must be made and if not made are waived unless excused by the court for good cause shown.

Rule 26(d), Timing and Sequence of Discovery. The first sentence of Rule 26(d) states that, except as authorized under the federal rules or by local rule, order, or agreement of the parties, a party may not seek discovery from any source before the parties have met and conferred as required by Rule 26(f). The remainder of the rule is unchanged—formal discovery may proceed as under the old rule.

Rule 26(f), Meeting of Counsel, Written Discovery Plan. Except in actions exempted by local rule or when otherwise ordered, parties must meet at least fourteen days before a Rule 16(b) scheduling conference is held or a scheduling order is due to:

- discuss the nature and basis of their claims and defenses and the possibility of settlement;
- make or arrange to make the disclosures required by Rule 26(a)(1); and
- develop a written discovery plan, which must be submitted to the court within 10 days of the meeting.

Using the Attached Tables to Understand Courts' Responses to FRCP 26 and the Courts' Requirements Concerning Disclosure

Table 1 presents the courts' responses to Rule 26(a)(1)-(3) and Table 2 describes their responses to Rule 26(d) and (f). The information in the tables is derived from several sources. In anticipation of or subsequent to promulgation of the amended federal rules, nearly two-thirds of the districts issued orders, notices, or local rule revisions identifying which of the federal rule amendments would take effect in the district. These courts are marked by an asterisk next to their names. For a substantial number of districts, as noted in the column on the far right in both tables, the decision is temporary, awaiting either more study or approval of proposed local rule changes.[3]

For courts that did not issue written responses to the federal rule amendments, we spoke with the clerk of court or, in a few instances, other court staff to obtain information about the court's disclosure and discovery requirements. In a number of these courts the federal rules are fully in effect and the court found no need to say so officially. For several others, particularly several exempting cases from the Rule 26 requirements, the CJRA plan or local rules or orders that pre-date the federal rule changes either explicitly take precedence or are presumed to do so, and therefore the court issued no official response to the federal rule changes.[4]

For districts that have decided, either temporarily or for the longer term, *not* to implement one of the requirements of Rule 26(a), (d), and (f), we examined the CJRA plan and local rules to see whether either one has requirements similar to the federal

---

[3] I appreciate the assistance of Kirkland and Ellis (Washington, DC office), who collected many of the orders and kindly shared them with me. Thanks go as well to Abel Mattos and Mark Shapiro at the Administrative Office of the United States Courts, who worked with me to collect the remainder.

[4] The authority of CJRA plans vis-a-vis local or federal rules is an open question, but most courts consider their plans to have the same force as these rules. The degree of authority becomes problematic when the plan is in conflict with either local or federal rules. Some courts specify which takes precedence, but many do not.

rule. A number of courts, for example, included disclosure provisions in CJRA plans adopted well before the federal rules were amended. Some of these courts were reluctant, when the amended federal rules went into effect, to change requirements already well established in their districts. Others who adopted plans late in 1993 anticipated promulgation of the federal rule amendments and addressed these expected changes in their plans. Thus, for courts opting out of one or more of the federal rule requirements covered by these tables, we have tried to indicate whether a similar requirement exists in local rules or CJRA plans. This information may be found in the second column from the right in each table. Without this information, it is easy to underestimate the number of courts with disclosure provisions.[5]

The tables can be used, then, in two ways: first, to determine how the courts have implemented specific amendments of Rule 26 and, second, to determine whether any form of disclosure is in effect in a particular court.

Short summaries of dense, technical information, such as rules, can do violence to the nuances of that information. These tables are no different. They provide only limited information, for example, about the types of cases or information subject to disclosure requirements. They also do not reveal the extent to which individual judges apply disclosure requirements. In using the tables, please read the footnotes carefully, as they provide important definitions and cautions regarding the information in the tables. In general, the tables are best used as an overview of the courts' responses to amended Rule 26 and their disclosure requirements. Users who need to know specific requirements—for example, attorneys handling cases in federal court—should not rely on these tables nor cite them as legal authority.

A Summary Description of the Courts' Responses to Amended FRCP 26(a) and of the Courts' Disclosure Requirements

One of the principal conclusions to be drawn from Table 1 is that classifying courts as "opting in" and "opting out" of Rule 26's disclosure requirements greatly oversimplifies the courts' responses to amended Rule 26 and understates the extent to which parties will encounter disclosure requirements in federal courts. Simple summaries also do not show that the issue is unsettled in many courts: Over a third of the districts have not yet made a decision or have made only a provisional one.

Yet a general picture of disclosure can be drawn, and in the table below we have sketched out one way of doing this. Note that a few courts whose status is ambiguous are not included in the table and therefore the numbers do not add to 94. Note, too, that considerable judgment must be used in classifying some courts; others might classify specific courts differently than we have. With those caveats, the table below summarizes the courts' responses to amended FRCP 26(a) and the extent to which disclosure will be required in the federal courts.

---

[5] I am grateful to Melissa Pecherski, Mia Kim, and Jane Ganz, colleagues in the Research Division, for their assistance in reviewing local rules and CJRA plans.

Summary of Courts' Responses to Amended FRCP 26(a) and of Courts' Disclosure Requirements

Nature of the Court's Response	Number of Courts
Courts whose decisions are final[1] and where FRCP 26(a) is in effect	**32**
Courts whose decisions are final[1] and where FRCP 26(a) is not in effect	**6**
(a)(1) only is not in effect	4
Courts whose decisions are final[1] and where FRCP 26(a) is not in effect but that have other provisions for disclosure	**21**
The individual judge is explicitly given authority to require disclosure	13[2]
Local rules or the CJRA plan require disclosure	8[3]
Courts whose decisions are provisional	**30**
FRCP 26(a) provisionally *is not* in effect	25
(a)(1) only is provisionally not in effect	12
Local requirements are in place[4]	6
(a)(1)-(3) are provisionally not in effect	13
Local requirements are in place[4]	2
FRCP 26(a) provisionally *is* in effect	5

---

1 In one sense no such decision is final, since courts periodically review and may revise local rules and procedures. But in this context we are describing these decisions as final in contrast to courts that have specifically stated that their decisions are provisional or temporary pending further study of the federal rule amendments.

2 Of these thirteen courts, four are not implementing (a)(1)-(3) and nine are not implementing only (a)(1).

3 Of these eight courts, six are not implementing (a)(1)-(3) and two are not implementing only (a)(1).

4 The court's local rules, general orders, or CJRA plan require disclosure.

This table shows, first, that Rule 26(a)(1), which requires initial disclosure, has been rejected more often than the other disclosure subsections of the rule. Altogether, 52 courts have exempted cases from the requirements of Rule 26(a)(1). Of these, however, sixteen require disclosure through local rules or orders or the CJRA plan, and thirteen specifically give individual judges authority to require initial disclosure. Further, 25 of the 52 courts have not yet made a final decision. If the provisional decisions become permanent and if local rules and plans remain in effect, cases in 23 courts would be exempt from any rules—federal or local—requiring initial disclosure. Cases in thirteen of these courts would also be exempt from expert and pretrial disclosure.

On the other hand—and, again, if current decisions regarding the federal rule amendments hold and if local disclosure requirements continue in effect—in two-thirds of the courts parties may face initial disclosure requirements: 32 courts where the federal rules are fully in effect and 34 courts where the local rules or CJRA plan require it or the individual judge may order it.

At this time few of the fifteen largest districts, as measured by number of judgeships, are fully implementing Rule 26(a). The table below shows that among the fifteen courts with twelve or more judgeships, the most common response appears to be a preference for local rules or for judicial discretion in application of the federal rule. A third, however, have not yet made a decision.

Implementation of Amended FRCP 26(a) in the Fifteen Largest Courts*

Full implementation of FRCP 26(a)	3
Local rule or CJRA plan requires disclosure	3
26(a)(1) not in effect unless ordered by judge	4
26(a)(1) not in effect while final decision is pending	2
26(a)(1)-(3) not in effect while final decision is pending	2
No decision made to date	1

* Courts with twelve or more judgeships

In general, the tables—and particularly Table 1—reveal a complicated picture. Not only do nearly a third of the courts have yet to make a final decision regarding implementation of Rule 26, but among the two-thirds that have decided a variety of requirements will be found. In nearly half of these the federal rule is fully in effect. In most of the others, the requirements will depend on local rules or on the requirements of the individual judge.

TABLE 1

FEDERAL DISTRICT COURT IMPLEMENTATION OF DISCLOSURE[1]

March 1, 1994

District[2]	Provisions of FRCP 26(a) (1)-(3) that are in effect[3]	Provisions of FRCP 26(a)(1)-(3) that are not in effect[4]	Other disclosure requirements in effect in courts not following one or more provisions of FRCP 26(a)(1)-(3)[5]	Court has not yet made decision or has made only a provisional decision
AL-M*	26(a)(2)(A) & (C) and (a)(3) are in effect.	26(a)(1) and (a)(2)(B) are not in effect at this time.		Advisory group will study 26(a)(1)-(2) further and make recommendations.
AL-N*	All[6]			
AL-S		No explicit rejection, but 26(a)(1)-(3) are not in effect at this time.		Court will make final decision within next few months.
AK	All			
AZ	All			
AR-E*	All			
AR-W*		26(a)(1)-(3) are not in effect, unless ordered by the judge in the specific case.		

Table 1: Federal District Court Implementation of Disclosure
Research Division, Federal Judicial Center, March 1, 1994

District	Provisions of FRCP 26(a) (1)-(3) that are in effect	Provisions of FRCP 26(a)(1)-(3) that are not in effect	Other disclosure requirements in effect in courts not following one or more provisions of FRCP 26(a)	Court has not yet made decision or has made only a provisional decision
CA-C*	26(a)(2)(A) & (B) are in effect.	26(a)(1), 26(a)(2)(C), and 26(a)(3) are deferred until June 1, 1994.	Local rule requires exchange of documents that support own contentions.	Court will make final decision by June 1.
CA-E*		26(a)(1)-(3) are not in effect.	New local rule permits judge to order in specific case.	
CA-N*		No explicit rejection, but a general order on case management appears to take precedence.	General order, similar to the federal rule, provides for initial and expert disclosure.	
CA-S*		26(a)(1)-(3) are not in effect at this time.		Final decision awaits advisory group report on April 1.
CO*	Proposed local rules adopt all.			Final decision awaits approval of proposed local rules.
CT*		26(a)(1)-(3) are not in effect at this time.		Court will study the matter further.
DE*	26(a)(2) & (3) are in effect.	26(a)(1) is not in effect at this time.	Local rule requires initial disclosure in certain case types.	Court will study the matter further.
DC*	All			
FL-M*	26(a)(2) & (3) are in effect.	26(a)(1) is not in effect.		

**Table 1: Federal District Court Implementation of Disclosure
Research Division, Federal Judicial Center, March 1, 1994**

District	Provisions of FRCP 26(a) (1)-(3) that are in effect	Provisions of FRCP 26(a)(1)-(3) that are not in effect	Other disclosure requirements in effect in courts not following one or more provisions of FRCP 26(a)	Court has not yet made decision or has made only a provisional decision
FL-N	All			
FL-S			Local rules require exchange of documents and witnesses, as well as expert disclosure.	Decision not yet made.
GA-M	All			
GA-N			CJRA plan requires completion by each party of standard interrogatories.	Decision not yet made.
GA-S	All			
GU	All			
HI*		26(a)(1)-(3) are not in effect at this time.		Decision will be made in a "reasonable" time.
ID*	26(a)(3) is in effect.	When in conflict, local rules will supersede 26(a)(1)-(2) until final decision is made.	Local rule, similar to the federal rule, requires initial disclosure.	Final decision postponed until April.
IL-C*	All			

3

Table 1: Federal District Court Implementation of Disclosure Research Division, Federal Judicial Center, March 1, 1994

District	Provisions of FRCP 26(a)(1)-(3) that are in effect	Provisions of FRCP 26(a)(1)-(3) that are not in effect	Other disclosure requirements in effect in courts not following one or more provisions of FRCP 26(a)	Court has not yet made decision or has made only a provisional decision
IL-N*	26(a)(2)&(3) are in effect.	26(a)(1) is not in effect except as ordered by the judge in the specific case.	CJRA plan permits judges to apply 26(a)(1) on a case-by-case basis.	
IL-S	All			
IN-N		No explicit rejection, but CJRA plan takes precedence.	CJRA plan includes experimentation with disclosure.	
IN-S*	26(a)(2)&(3) are in effect.	Proposed local rules, in effect as emergency rules, exempt cases from 26(a)(1) and instruct parties to consider in their case management plans whether 26(a)(2)(B) should be varied by parties' stipulation.		Final decision awaits close of comment period on proposed local rules.
IA-N*	Proposed local rules adopt 26(a)(1)(C)&(D), (a)(2)(A), and (a)(3).	Proposed local rules, to be effective June 1, '94 if approved, will exempt cases from 26(a)(1)(A)&(B) and (a)(2)(B)&(C). These federal rules are not in effect in the meantime.		Final decision awaits close of comment period on proposed local rules.
IA-S*	Proposed local rules adopt 26(a)(1)(C)&(D), (a)(2)(A), and (a)(3).	Proposed local rules, to be effective June 1, '94 if approved, will exempt cases from 26(a)(1)(A)&(B) and (a)(2)(B)&(C). These federal rules are not in effect in the meantime.		Final decision awaits close of comment period on proposed local rules.

Table 1: Federal District Court Implementation of Disclosure
Research Division, Federal Judicial Center, March 1, 1994

District	Provisions of FRCP 26(a)(1)-(3) that are in effect	Provisions of FRCP 26(a)(1)-(3) that are not in effect	Other disclosure requirements in effect in courts not following one or more provisions of FRCP 26(a)	Court has not yet made decision or has made only a provisional decision
KS*	All			
KY-E	All			
KY-W	All			
LA-E*	26(a)(2)&(3) are in effect.	26(a)(1) is not in effect unless ordered by the judge in the specific case.	CJRA plan permits judge to establish disclosure requirements on a case-by-case basis at initial scheduling conference.	
LA-M*	26(a)(2)&(3) are in effect.	26(a)(1) is not in effect unless ordered by the judge in the specific case.	Proposed local rule amendments permit judge to order initial disclosure in the specific case. CJRA plan controls timing of expert and pretrial disclosure.	
LA-W*	26(a)(2)&(3) are in effect.	26(a)(1) is not in effect unless ordered by the judge in the specific case.	Amended local rule permits judge to order initial disclosure in the specific case.	
ME*	26(a)(2)&(3) are in effect.	26(a)(1) is not in effect.		
MD*	26(a)(2)&(3) are in effect.	26(a)(1) is not in effect, except for a limited number of case types.		

Table 1: Federal District Court Implementation of Disclosure
Research Division, Federal Judicial Center, March 1, 1994

District	Provisions of FRCP 26(a)(1)-(3) that are in effect	Provisions of FRCP 26(a)(1)-(3) that are not in effect	Other disclosure requirements in effect in courts not following one or more provisions of FRCP 26(a)	Court has not yet made decision or has made only a provisional decision
MA		26(a)(1)-(3) are not in effect.	Local rules require initial document disclosure. CJRA plan permits judge to order disclosure in the specific case.	
MI-E*		26(a)(1)-(3) are not in effect before April 1, 1994 or until further ordered.		Final decision will be made later.
MI-W*	26(a)(2)&(3) are in effect.	26(a)(1) is not in effect.	Local rules permit judge to order initial disclosure in the specific case. CJRA plan and local rules govern expert and pretrial disclosure.	
MN	All, subject to application by judge in the specific case.			
MS-N		No explicit rejection, but CJRA plan takes precedence.	CJRA plan provides for disclosure similar to federal rule.	
MS-S		No explicit rejection, but CJRA plan takes precedence.	CJRA plan provides for disclosure similar to federal rule.	
MO-E*	26(a)(2)&(3) are in effect.	26(a)(1) is not in effect.	Administrative order permits judge to determine the appropriate amount of disclosure in the specific case.	
MO-W	All			

Table 1: Federal District Court Implementation of Disclosure Research Division, Federal Judicial Center, March 1, 1994

District	Provisions of FRCP 26(a) (1)-(3) that are in effect	Provisions of FRCP 26(a)(1)-(3) that are not in effect	Other disclosure requirements in effect in courts not following one or more provisions of FRCP 26(a)	Court has not yet made decision or has made only a provisional decision
MT*	All			
NE*	All			
NV*	26(a)(2)(A) & (C) and (a)(3) are in effect.	26(a)(1) and (a)(2)(B) are not in effect at this time.		Will study further.
NH*		26(a)(1)-(3) are not in effect at this time.		Will study further.
NJ*	All			
NM*	All			
NY-E*		26(a)(1)-(3) are not in effect at this time.	CJRA plan, similar to the federal rule, requires initial disclosure.	Will study further.
NY-N*		26(a)(1)-(3) are not in effect at this time.		Will study further.
NY-S*		26(a)(1)-(3) are not in effect at this time.		Will study further.

Table 1: Federal District Court Implementation of Disclosure Research Division, Federal Judicial Center, March 1, 1994

District	Provisions of FRCP 26(a)(1)-(3) that are in effect	Provisions of FRCP 26(a)(1)-(3) that are not in effect	Other disclosure requirements in effect in courts not following one or more provisions of FRCP 26(a)	Court has not yet made decision or has made only a provisional decision
NY-W*		26(a)(1)-(3) are not in effect.		
NC-E*	All			
NC-M*	26(a)(2) &(3) are in effect.	26(a)(1) is not in effect.		
NC-W	All			
ND*	All			
NMI			CJRA plan, similar to the federal rule, requires initial, expert, and pretrial disclosure.	Unknown.
OH-N	All			
OH-S*	26(a)(2) &(3) are in effect.	26(a)(1) is not in effect unless ordered by judge in specific case.		
OK-E*	26(a)(1)(D) and (a)(3) are in effect.	26(a)(1)(A)-(C) and 26(a)(2) are not in effect.	CJRA plan requires disclosure of factual and legal basis for the claim.	

Table 1: Federal District Court Implementation of Disclosure Research Division, Federal Judicial Center, March 1, 1994

District	Provisions of FRCP 26(a) (1)-(3) that are in effect	Provisions of FRCP 26(a)(1)-(3) that are not in effect	Other disclosure requirements in effect in courts not following one or more provisions of FRCP 26(a)	Court has not yet made decision or has made only a provisional decision
OK-N*	26(a)(1)(D), 26(a)(2), and 26(a)(3) are in effect.	26(a)(1)(A)-(C) are not in effect.	CJRA plan permits judge to order initial disclosure in the specific case.	
OK-W*	26(a)(2) &(3) are in effect.	26(a)(1) is not in effect at this time.	Amended local rule requires disclosure of experts, documents, and insurance agreements.	Will further study the new federal rules.
OR*	26(a)(2) &(3) are in effect.	26(a)(1) is not in effect at this time.	Interim local rule permits judge to order initial disclosure in the specific case.	Final outcome awaiting decision on interim local rules.
PA-E*	26(a)(2) &(3) are in effect.	26(a)(1) is not in effect at this time.	Local rules, similar to the federal rule, require initial disclosure.	Court will further evaluate 26(a)(1).
PA-M*	All			
PA-W*	26(a)(2) &(3) are in effect.	26(a)(1) is not in effect at this time.		Will study matter further.
PR	All			
RI	All			

Table 1: Federal District Court Implementation of Disclosure Research Division, Federal Judicial Center, March 1, 1994

District	Provisions of FRCP 26(a)(1)-(3) that are in effect	Provisions of FRCP 26(a)(1)-(3) that are not in effect	Other disclosure requirements in effect in courts not following one or more provisions of FRCP 26(a)	Court has not yet made decision or has made only a provisional decision
SC*	26(a)(2)(A) and (a)(3) are in effect.	26(a)(1) and 26(a)(2)(B)-(C) are not in effect.	Local rule requires completion by each party of standard interrogatories and requires some initial disclosure.	
SD*	All			
TN-E	All			
TN-M*	26(a)(2) &(3) are in effect.	26(a)(1) is not in effect.	CJRA plan permits judge to order initial disclosure in the specific case.	
TN-W*	All			Will reconsider after six months (mid-summer 1994).
TX-E		No explicit rejection, but 26(a)(1)-(3) are not in effect.	CJRA plan and local rules, similar to the federal rule, require initial, expert, and pretrial disclosure.	
TX-N*		Court will not at this time uniformly abrogate, modify, or exercise its options under the amended rules.	Special order permits judges to apply the amended rules as they deem appropriate.	Final decision postponed while court studies matter.
TX-S*	All			

10

Table 1: Federal District Court Implementation of Disclosure Research Division, Federal Judicial Center, March 1, 1994

District	Provisions of FRCP 26(a) (1)-(3) that are in effect	Provisions of FRCP 26(a)(1)-(3) that are not in effect	Other disclosure requirements in effect in courts not following one or more provisions of FRCP 26(a)	Court has not yet made decision or has made only a provisional decision
TX-W*		26(a)(1)-(3) are not in effect.	CJRA plan requires initial and expert disclosure.	
UT	In effect on individual judge basis pending final decision.			Final decision to be made later.
VT*		26(a)(1)-(3) are not in effect at this time.		Decision postponed while court studies matter.
VI			CJRA plan, similar to the federal rule, requires initial and expert disclosure.	Decision not yet made.
VA-E*	26(a)(2)&(3) are in effect.	26(a)(1) is not in effect.		
VA-W	All			
WA-E		No explicit rejection, but 26(a)(1)-(3) are not in effect at this time.		Final decision postponed.
WA-W*		26(a)(1)-(3) are not in effect at this time.		Final decision postponed.

Table 1: Federal District Court Implementation of Disclosure Research Division, Federal Judicial Center, March 1, 1994

District	Provisions of FRCP 26(a) (1)-(3) that are in effect	Provisions of FRCP 26(a)(1)-(3) that are not in effect	Other disclosure requirements in effect in courts not following one or more provisions of FRCP 26(a)	Court has not yet made decision or has made only a provisional decision
WV-N			CJRA plan, similar to federal rule, provides for disclosure, but has not been implemented awaiting Congressional action on the proposed rules.	Will decide soon.
WV-S	In effect pending final decision.			Will decide soon.
WI-E*		26(a)(1)-(3) are not in effect.	Local rules require expert disclosure and completion by each party of standard interrogatories.	
WI-W*	All			
WY		No explicit rejection, but 26(a)(1)-(3) are not in effect at this time.	Local rule, similar to the federal rule, requires initial and expert disclosure.	Will decide in next few months.

---

[1] The information in the table is derived from orders and notices issued by the courts subsequent to or in anticipation of the federal rule amendments; from local rules; from CJRA plans; and from clerks of court or other court staff. See the introduction to these tables for a fuller discussion of the sources. The table should not be cited as legal authority nor substituted for a careful examination of federal rules or local rules, orders, and Civil Justice Reform Act plans.
[2] An asterisk next to a court's name indicates it has spoken formally in response to the federal rule changes—e.g., by issuing an order or by amending local rules. Absence of an asterisk means the court has not spoken formally on the federal rule amendments.
[3] Where the federal rule is in effect, the court may nonetheless use local rules or orders to alter the effect of the federal rule—e.g., by exempting such case types as habeas corpus, social security, and bankruptcy; setting different time frames for disclosure; requiring only documents in support of one's own contentions; or permitting individual judges to opt out. Local rules or orders may also establish an effective date later than December 1, 1993 and may specify whether the

Table 1: Federal District Court Implementation of Disclosure
Research Division, Federal Judicial Center, March 1, 1994

federal rules will be applied only to newly filed cases or also to pending cases. Note that some courts' orders in response to the federal rule changes are explicit only in stating which provisions are *rejected*. When the order does not specifically reject a provision, we assume it is in effect in the court.

[4] "Not in effect" means that cases filed in these courts are exempt from the requirements of the federal rule subdivisions listed in the column. In many courts, however, individual judges may require parties to follow the federal rule requirements, or local rules or CJRA plans may provide for some type of disclosure (see the next column).

[5] The courts with entries in this column have elected, either temporarily or for the longer term, to exempt cases from some or all of the disclosure provisions of FRCP 26(a), but they do provide for disclosure through their local rules or CJRA plan. Some of these courts have requirements similar to the federal rule, while others require much more limited disclosure or require none but permit judges to order it in the specific case. Where the entry says "similar to the federal rule", the local rule may be similar to an early version of the federal rule ("bears significantly on") or to the final version ("alleged with particularity"). Though similar, the local rule may differ in its particulars—e.g., the timing of disclosure, whether adverse material must be disclosed—but in general "similar" signifies that the court embraces the idea of and requires self-executing disclosure in some form.

[6] "All" indicates all three provisions under discussion here—26(a)(1)-(3)—are in effect, although, as explained in note 1, local rules or orders, as well as individual judges, may alter some of the requirements.

TABLE 2

FEDERAL DISTRICT COURT IMPLEMENTATION OF DISCOVERY DEFERMENT AND THE MEETING OF PARTIES[1]

MARCH 1, 1994

District[2]	FRCP 26(d)[3] (Timing and Sequence of Discovery)	FRCP 26(f) (Meeting of Parties)	Other requirements in effect in courts not following FRCP 26(d) or (f)	Court has not yet made decision or has made only a provisional decision
AL-M*	Discovery deferment is not in effect at this time.	Not in effect at this time.		Advisory group will study further and make recommendations.
AL-N*	In effect.	In effect.		
AL-S	Not in effect at this time.	Not in effect at this time.		Court will make final decision within next few months.
AK	In effect.	In effect.		
AZ	In effect.	In effect.		
AR-E*	In effect.	In effect.		
AR-W*	Discovery deferment is not in effect.	Not in effect.		
CA-C*	Decision postponed until 6/1/94.	In effect.		Court will make final decision by June 1.

Table 2: Federal District Court Implementation of Discovery Deferment and the Meeting of Parties
Research Division, Federal Judicial Center, March 1, 1994

District	FRCP 26(d) (Timing and Sequence of Discovery)	FRCP 26(f) (Meeting of Parties)	Other requirements in effect in courts not following FRCP 26(d) or (f)	Court has not yet made decision or has made only a provisional decision
CA-E*	Discovery deferment is not in effect.	Not in effect.		
CA-N*	No explicit rejection.	No explicit rejection.	General order includes requirements similar to federal rule.	
CA-S*	Not in effect at this time.	Not in effect at this time.		Final decision awaits advisory group report on April 1.
CO*	In effect.	In effect.		
CT*	Appears to be in effect.	Appears to be in effect.		
DE*	Not in effect at this time.	Not in effect at this time.		Court will study matter further.
DC*	In effect.	In effect.		
FL-M*	Appears to be in effect.	Appears to be in effect.		
FL-N	In effect.	In effect.		
FL-S	Not yet decided.	Not yet decided.		Decision not yet made.

Table 2: Federal District Court Implementation of Discovery Deferment and the Meeting of Parties
Research Division, Federal Judicial Center, March 1, 1994

District	FRCP 26(d) (Timing and Sequence of Discovery)	FRCP 26(f) (Meeting of Parties)	Other requirements in effect in courts not following FRCP 26(d) or (f)	Court has not yet made decision or has made only a provisional decision
GA-M	In effect.	In effect.		
GA-N	Not yet decided.	Not yet decided.		Decision not yet made.
GA-S	In effect.	In effect.		
GU	In effect.	In effect.		
HI*	Not in effect at this time.	Not in effect at this time.		Decision will be made in a "reasonable" time.
ID*	Appears to be mooted by non-implementation of 26(f).	Not in effect at this time.		Final decision postponed until April.
IL-C*	In effect.	In effect.		
IL-N*	In effect.	In effect.		
IL-S	In effect.	In effect.		
IN-N	No explicit rejection.	No explicit rejection.	CJRA plan includes experimentation with disclosure.	

Table 2: Federal District Court Implementation of Discovery Deferment and the Meeting of Parties Research Division, Federal Judicial Center, March 1, 1994

District	FRCP 26(d) (Timing and Sequence of Discovery)	FRCP 26(f) (Meeting of Parties)	Other requirements in effect in courts not following FRCP 26(d) or (f)	Court has not yet made decision or has made only a provisional decision
IN-S*	Not in effect at this time.	Not in effect at this time.		Final decision awaits close of comment period on proposed local rules.
IA-N*	In effect.	In effect.		
IA-S*	In effect.	In effect.		
KS*	In effect.	In effect.		
KY-E	In effect.	In effect.		
KY-W	In effect.	In effect.		
LA-E*	In effect.	In effect.		
LA-M*	In effect.	In effect.		
LA-W*	In effect.	In effect.		
ME*	Appears to be mooted by non-implementation of 26(f).	Not in effect.		

Table 2: Federal District Court Implementation of Discovery Deferment and the Meeting of Parties
Research Division, Federal Judicial Center, March 1, 1994

District	FRCP 26(d) (Timing and Sequence of Discovery)	FRCP 26(f) (Meeting of Parties)	Other requirements in effect in courts not following FRCP 26(d) or (f)	Court has not yet made decision or has made only a provisional decision
MD*	In effect in certain case types (appears to be more complex case types).	In effect in certain case types (appears to be more complex case types).		
MA	Appears not to be in effect.	Appears not to be in effect.		
MI-E*	Appears to be in effect.	Appears to be in effect.		
MI-W*	In effect.	In effect in conjunction with order setting Rule 16 conference.		
MN	Each judge decides for each case whether to apply the rule.	Each judge decides for each case whether to apply the rule.		
MS-N	No explicit rejection.	No explicit rejection.	CJRA plan includes requirements similar to federal rule.	
MS-S	No explicit rejection.	No explicit rejection.	CJRA plan includes requirements similar to federal rule.	
MO-E*	Appears to be in effect.	Appears to be in effect.		
MO-W	In effect.	In effect.		

5

Table 2: Federal District Court Implementation of Discovery Deferment and the Meeting of Parties Research Division, Federal Judicial Center, March 1, 1994

District	FRCP 26(d) (Timing and Sequence of Discovery)	FRCP 26(f) (Meeting of Parties)	Other requirements in effect in courts not following FRCP 26(d) or (f)	Court has not yet made decision or has made only a provisional decision
MT*	Deferment of discovery is not in effect unless otherwise ordered.	Not in effect unless otherwise ordered.		
NE*	In effect.	In effect.		
NV*	Appears to be mooted by non-implementation of 26(f).	Not in effect at this time.		Court will study matter further.
NH*	The parts referencing 26(a) and 26(f) are not in effect.	Not in effect.		
NJ*	In effect.	In effect.		
NM*	In effect.	In effect.		
NY-E*	Appears not to be in effect at this time.	Appears not to be in effect at this time.		Will study further.
NY-N*	Appears to be in effect.	Appears to be in effect.		
NY-S*	Appears to be in effect.	Appears to be in effect.		
NY-W*	Not in effect.	Not in effect.		

Table 2: Federal District Court Implementation of Discovery Deferment and the Meeting of Parties Research Division, Federal Judicial Center, March 1, 1994

District	FRCP 26(d) (Timing and Sequence of Discovery)	FRCP 26(f) (Meeting of Parties)	Other requirements in effect in courts not following FRCP 26(d) or (f)	Court has not yet made decision or has made only a provisional decision
NC-E*	In effect.	In effect.		
NC-M*	In effect.	In effect.		
NC-W	In effect.	In effect.		
ND*	In effect.	In effect.		
NMI	Unknown.	Unknown.		Unknown.
OH-N	In effect.	In effect.		
OH-S*	Not in effect.	Not in effect.		
OK-E*	Not in effect.	In effect.		
OK-N*	Discovery deferment is not in effect.	In effect.		
OK-W*	Not clear from order.	Not clear from order.		Will further study the new federal rules.

Table 2: Federal District Court Implementation of Discovery Deferment and the Meeting of Parties
Research Division, Federal Judicial Center, March 1, 1994

District	FRCP 26(d) (Timing and Sequence of Discovery)	FRCP 26(f) (Meeting of Parties)	Other requirements in effect in courts not following FRCP 26(d) or (f)	Court has not yet made decision or has made only a provisional decision
OR*	Discovery deferment is not in effect at this time.	Not in effect at this time.		Final outcome awaiting decision on interim local rules.
PA-E*	Discovery deferment is not in effect at this time.	Not in effect at this time.	Discovery deferment and discovery plan required by CJRA plan.	Court will further evaluate 26(d) and (f).
PA-M*	In effect.	In effect.		
PA-W*	Discovery deferment is not in effect at this time.	Not in effect at this time.		Court will study matter further.
PR	In effect.	In effect.		
RI	In effect.	In effect.		
SC*	Discovery deferment is not in effect.	Not in effect.		
SD*	In effect.	In effect.		
TN-E	In effect.	In effect.		
TN-M*	Not clear from order.	Not clear from order.		

Table 2: Federal District Court Implementation of Discovery Deferment and the Meeting of Parties Research Division, Federal Judicial Center, March 1, 1994

District	FRCP 26(d) (Timing and Sequence of Discovery)	FRCP 26(f) (Meeting of Parties)	Other requirements in effect in courts not following FRCP 26(d) or (f)	Court has not yet made decision or has made only a provisional decision
TN-W*	In effect at this time.	In effect at this time.		Will reconsider decision after six months (mid-summer 1994).
TX-E	No explicit rejection.	No explicit rejection.	CJRA plan includes requirements similar to federal rule.	
TX-N*	Application of rule is at discretion of each judge.	Application of rule is at discretion of each judge.		Decision postponed while court studies matter.
TX-S*	In effect.	In effect.		
TX-W*	Not in effect.	Not in effect.		
UT	In effect on individual judge basis pending final decision.	In effect on individual judge basis pending final decision.		Final decision postponed.
VT*	Appears to be in effect.	Appears to be in effect.		
VI				Decision not yet made.
VA-E*	Discovery deferment is not in effect.	Not in effect.		
VA-W	In effect.	In effect.		

9

Table 2: Federal District Court Implementation of Discovery Deferment and the Meeting of Parties Research Division, Federal Judicial Center, March 1, 1994

District	FRCP 26(d) (Timing and Sequence of Discovery)	FRCP 26(f) (Meeting of Parties)	Other requirements in effect in courts not following FRCP 26(d) or (f)	Court has not yet made decision or has made only a provisional decision
WA-E	Not in effect at this time.	Not in effect at this time.	Written discovery plan required by local rule.	Decision postponed.
WA-W*	Not in effect at this time.	Not in effect at this time.		Decision postponed.
WV-N	Will decide soon.	Will decide soon.		Court will decide soon.
WV-S	In effect until final decision is made.	In effect until final decision made.		Court will decide soon.
WI-E*	Not in effect.	Not in effect.		
WI-W*	In effect.	In effect.		
WY	Not in effect at this time.	Not in effect at this time.		Will decide in next few months.

---

[1] The information in the table is derived from orders and notices issued by the courts subsequent to or in anticipation of the federal rule amendments; from local rules; from CJRA plans; and from clerks of court or other court staff. See the introduction to these tables for a fuller discussion of the sources. The table should not be cited as legal authority nor substituted for a careful examination of federal rules or local rules, orders, and Civil Justice Reform Act plans.
[2] An asterisk next to a court's name indicates it has spoken formally in response to the federal rule changes—e.g., through an order or by amending local rules. Absence of an asterisk means the court has not spoken formally on the federal rule amendments.
[3] Where the federal rule governs, the court may nonetheless use local rules or orders to alter the effect of the federal rule—e.g., by exempting certain case types. Local rules or orders may also establish an effective date later than December 1, 1993 and may specify whether the federal rules will be applied only to cases filed after the effective date of the rules or also to pending cases. Note that individual judges may also modify the requirements or exempt cases from them altogether. Note also that some courts' orders in response to the federal rule changes are explicit only in stating which provisions are *rejected*. When the order does not specifically reject a provision, we assume it is in effect in the court. We have designated these instances as "appears to be in effect."

www.ingramcontent.com/pod-product-compliance
Lightning Source LLC
Chambersburg PA
CBHW080532190526
45169CB00008B/3130